Dominic

A Mother's Grief

Rosie Lambert

Copyright © 2013 Rosie Lambert

The moral right of the author has been asserted.

Apart from any fair dealing for the purposes of research or private study, or criticism or review, as permitted under the Copyright, Designs and Patents Act 1988, this publication may only be reproduced, stored or transmitted, in any form or by any means, with the prior permission in writing of the publishers, or in the case of reprographic reproduction in accordance with the terms of licences issued by the Copyright Licensing Agency. Enquiries concerning reproduction outside those terms should be sent to the publishers.

Matador
9 Priory Business Park,
Wistow Road, Kibworth Beauchamp,
Leicestershire. LE8 0RX
Tel: (+44) 116 279 2299
Fax: (+44) 116 279 2277
Email: books@troubador.co.uk
Web: www.troubador.co.uk/matador

ISBN 9781783062171

British Library Cataloguing in Publication Data.
A catalogue record for this book is available from the British Library.

Typeset by Troubador Publishing Ltd, Leicester, UK
Printed and bound in the UK by TJ International, Padstow, Cornwall

Matador is an imprint of Troubador Publishing Ltd

For Dominic, thank you for touching my life. You were here so briefly, but your existence has had such a lasting impact. Know that you will always be loved.

For my husband, Mick and my sons, Ryan and Adam for all their support and for putting up with my grumpiness from burning the midnight oil trying to get this book finished.

ACKNOWLEDGEMENTS

Thanks to my parents and sister for always being there.

Thanks to Yvie for being such a good friend, especially during those first few months after Dominic died.

Thank you to Heather for recognising a need and doing something about it by founding SPRING and providing care and support to bereaved families, which otherwise would be sadly lacking.

And finally a special thank you to Kim, who became a close friend after we met at the first support meeting I went to, and to Cindy (SPRING counsellor), for their support, listening, honesty, constructive comments and advice, and for helping me to turn a bunch of poems into a proper book.

CONTENTS

Prologue — xi

PART 1

Dominic	2
Contradiction	3
Don't Tell Me	4
If Only	5
Imagination	6
The Pain of Grief	7
Existing	8
Depression	9
Head above Water	10
The Storm	11
Memories	12
Numb	13
Release	14
Insomnia	15
Alone	16
Dreams	17
Expectations	18
Trying to Let Go	19
The Mask	20
Lost Girl	21

PART 2

The Angel and the Devil	24
The Angel and the Devil – part II	25
Insanity	26
The Wound	27
Sometimes	28
Little Teddy Bear	29
The Onion	30
The Journey	31
Wishing	33
Always	34
The Future	35

PART 3

Reflections	38
Another Baby	39
A New Arrival	40
Time	41
Each New Day	42
A Christmas Message	43
Christmas Wishes	44
Alone at Christmas	45
Angel Wings	46

PART 4

The SPRING Suite	48
SPRING Open Support Meetings	49
Counselling	50
The Snowdrop Garden	51

Snowdrop Walk	52
Wave of Light	53
Christmas Service	54
Cindy	55

PART 5

My Brother	58
One of Many	59
Precious Bundle	60
To Love Your Child	61
Epilogue	63

PROLOGUE

Dominic was born 14th December 2001 at 17 weeks and 4 days gestation. During my pregnancy I was quite sick; I was in and out of hospital for a couple of months with a condition called hyperemesis gravidarum, or in English, severe morning sickness. Even though this wasn't pleasant, it was tolerable because I knew I was going to end up with a new baby and I would definitely stop being sick when he was born, if not before.

Life was challenging at this stage because we were in the process of moving house and my oldest son, Ryan was just coming up to three. With me stuck in hospital, my poor husband ended up running around like a headless chicken trying to juggle our child, work, visiting and packing. It's a wonder he didn't have a nervous breakdown! I left hospital on Thursday 6th December, we moved house on Friday 7th and on Saturday 8th I stopped being sick. Things were improving and I was looking forward to getting well again, enjoying the second half of my pregnancy and settling into my new house.

A visit to the midwife a couple of days later ended up with a precautionary scan being booked because she couldn't hear the baby's heartbeat. We went for the scan on 13th December and that's when my world fell apart – there was no heartbeat. My baby had died. That wasn't part of my plan at all. I couldn't get my head around it; it didn't seem real. I kept hoping I would wake up, but it wasn't a dream. All I could think was, "why?"

Dominic was born in the Bereavement Suite at Poole Maternity Hospital. It was a brand new suite and we were the first family to use it. I was given some information leaflets whilst I was in the hospital. One of them was offering counselling through a charity called SPRING, which supports parents and relatives through baby loss. I didn't think I needed counselling, but my attention was drawn to the fact that the counsellor was also a midwife. I decided to phone because I hoped she might be able to answer some of my questions. I booked an appointment for the beginning of January and that was my introduction to counselling and SPRING.

It was only when I went for my first counselling session that I found out the bereavement suite existed purely because SPRING had raised the funds to put it in place. It soon became clear to me that SPRING was providing an invaluable service for people in my situation struggling to come to terms with the loss of a baby.

I only have one scan picture of Dominic; no photographs, hand or foot prints. This has been one of the hardest things for me to come to terms with over the years. I know that what's happened can never be changed, no matter how much you long for it to be different. I'm not good at outwardly expressing my feelings so I tend to bottle everything up and tell myself that I'm fine even when deep inside I know that I'm not.

About a month after Dominic was born I wrote a poem in his memory. I only ever meant to write one, but as time passed I found that poetry was the one true way I could express myself and let my feelings and grief out. My computer didn't pass judgement or feel sorry for me. I just sat in front of the screen for hours trying to process and understand my emotions.

I have shared some of my poetry with other bereaved parents and written poems specifically in relation to events organised by SPRING. I am often asked whether I have considered publishing them, so I've finally done it. If you have lost someone important in your life, then I hope you will be able to relate to my words and my journey. If they help you in any way then I will take comfort knowing that Dominic has made a difference and left his tiny footprint on the world.

PART 1

This first section starts with my original poem for Dominic. It covers the raw pain and grief I felt as I struggled to deal with my loss.

The healing process is not linear; sometimes you feel worse for no apparent reason or guilty because you've been feeling better. We are very good at putting pressure on ourselves of how we think we should be feeling, instead of allowing ourselves to be sad for our loss or happy because of other things in our lives.

DOMINIC

You are my child, a part of me
Your life cut so short, the world you didn't see
You were so tiny, held in my hand
Why you had to go, I don't understand

No chance for me to show my love
You've left this place for one above
I hope in your heart you can forgive
I let you down, you didn't live

It is so hard to sleep at night
I can't let go, there is no light
I feel the tears behind my eyes
It hurts so bad, I just can't cry

I want you with me, so very much
But now I'll never feel your touch
I'll never get to see you smile
It makes me wonder if it's all worthwhile

I need a reason I can believe
To ease the pain, then I can grieve
But nothing can stop me wondering why
It was you, my baby, who had to die

I know deep inside that life still goes on
For all those I love, I will be strong
Because although your life's been taken from me
In my heart you'll always be a precious memory

CONTRADICTION

Too small for hand and foot prints
Yet big enough to be born
Too small to take a photograph
But you had a perfect form

Too old to be a miscarriage
Too young to register your birth
Officially you don't exist
You don't have any worth

It seems so very harsh to me
The way we draw a line
You are still my baby
And that won't change with time

Who has the right to push you away
As if you didn't matter
If you weren't big enough to love
Why has my world been shattered

DON'T TELL ME

Don't tell me it's ok
Don't tell me I'll be fine
Don't tell me I'll get over it
That all it takes is time

Don't tell me I'm not crazy
Don't tell me how I should feel
Don't tell me it gets better
Because it still doesn't seem real

Don't tell me there's a reason
Don't tell me it was meant to be
Don't tell me that I'm strong enough
Please just be there for me

I'm not ready to accept
I just need you to listen
And put your arm around my shoulders
When in my eyes, tears start to glisten

IF ONLY

My special little baby, I want you to know
I'm so very sorry that I failed you so
When you were born, I should have held you tight
But I backed away, in my own shock and fright

If only I'd realised what little time we'd together
I should have cherished each second forever
If only I'd been stronger when you were taken away
To say that I wanted you back with me to stay

If only I'd wept for you, because you were gone
I couldn't do that, I was trying to be strong
But it wasn't for you, it was just for me
To hide all the pain, where no one could see

I wish so, so much that your photo was taken
If I thought I didn't need it, I was so mistaken
When they said for a picture, you were too small
If only I'd insisted, not played it cool

I don't want your forgiveness, I let you down
I want to wallow in self pity, but hope I don't drown
If only I'd had the courage, to let the world see my pain
Perhaps now I wouldn't feel like I'm going insane

If someone had told me, another chance could never be
For me to hold you and show you what you mean to me
If only somebody had held open the door
I could have been stronger, I could have had so much more

I'm scared as time passes, your face I'll forget
Because of my actions, I have so much regret
I couldn't think straight, I was blinded with pain
But what I wouldn't give to have our day again

IMAGINATION

Imagination can be so cruel
It can make me feel like a total fool
So many thoughts going round in my mind
So many feelings I can't leave behind

I hoped beyond hope, it was all a mistake
When you lay in my arms, I was sure you would wake
I imagined you looking up into my eyes
And the wondrous sound, when a baby first cries

Sometimes I believe that you're still alive
Put my hand to my stomach to feel you inside
The pain is so blinding, when reality hits
It sends me straight to the bottom of a bottomless pit

I imagine the future, if I'd only been stronger
You would be here now, your life so much longer
My body has failed in its one major task
Was to let you have life really so much to ask

All of these thoughts are completely in vain
But that won't stop me thinking them over again
It doesn't seem to matter how hard I have tried
I can't imagine life's meaning, now that you've died

THE PAIN OF GRIEF

My heart is so heavy, feels like it's torn out
It's almost stopped beating, because you're not about
I can hardly function, can't seem to move on
Because you're not here with me, where you belong

Feels like I've been kicked, something's pulling me down
I'm constantly fighting, should I give in and drown
Perhaps I should suffer, for letting you die
I don't have a reason, I'll never know why

I feel so, so guilty, that you didn't survive
I can blame only me, because you're not alive
I will live with these thoughts, until time runs out
But the strength of my love for you, don't ever doubt

I'm too scared to cry, can't lose my control
I don't want to spiral down such a black hole
If I keep falling down, will I ever come back
Best not to let myself come off the track

At times I want nothing but to wallow in pain
I can't give in, I'll go completely insane
It's all so consuming, where do I start
Should I let my head rule, or go with my heart

Sometimes I wonder if I'll ever pull through
And then I think that I don't deserve to
If I ask for forgiveness, I'm pitying myself
I can't justify that, I've still got my health

I'm trying so hard, to be brave and strong
But all I can think is where did I go wrong
It's only because there are others I love
That my life is worth living, or I'd join you above

EXISTING

I can't think straight, when I try I can't breathe
I can't cry for you, I won't let myself grieve
I'm in a state of emotional suspense
Where nothing at all makes any sense
I can't even feel the pain anymore
Just consuming numbness that spreads through my core
I can't give in, feels like I'm barely alive
Engulfed in self-pity, I'm losing my drive
I hate that I can't stop myself from just existing this way
It makes it so hard just to get through the day

DEPRESSION

Don't know what to do with myself, nothing feels right
I'm surrounded by darkness, I can't find the light
It's all too much effort, don't want to get out of bed
Or I'll have to face reality, and that messes with my head

The emptiness inside, the feeling of despair
Unable to accept, can't show that you care
The lack of self confidence, doubt of your own mind
Belief that you're crazy, scared what probing will find

I question if it would be easier, to not be around
Long to lose the gloomy shroud that's weighing me down
Don't know what to do, or which way to turn
Just pray for the day that normality will return

So fickle is the nature of my mood swings
So easily affected by ordinary everyday things
I can't believe it will last, when I'm feeling ok
And I hate the self-pity, but it won't go away

Time drags its heels as I'm stuck in this rut
I don't know what's right, I can't trust my gut
I'm not living my life, just existing each day
I can't take this much more, I must find my way

HEAD ABOVE WATER

Sometimes it seems such a struggle
Just to keep myself afloat
My head keeps dipping under
I need to find a boat

I'm paddling like fury
Hoping to catch a glimpse of land
Just a little ray of hope
To give me the strength to stand

Can't succumb to the murky depths
But it's awfully inviting
Just to let it pull you down
Instead of continually fighting

Luckily I'm far too stubborn
I know that I will win
I know I have to help myself
So my future can begin

THE STORM

Menacing black clouds, day seems as dark as night
Thunder rumbles overhead, lightning forks as it strikes
Rain falling so hard, incessantly drumming on the ground
Almighty droplets pounding, drowning out all other sound
The storm's ferocity increasing, icy wind chilling to the bone
Keeping you a prisoner in the confines of your own home

The storm is violently raging, too severe to face head on
You know it has to pass, but you've endured it for so long
Gradually it weakens, a glimmer of sun peaks through the cloud
The howling wind is abating, the rain's drumming not so loud
Eventually it passes, the sky no longer so oppressive or as dark
But it's chaos that ensues, for the storm has really left its mark

MEMORIES

I want to hold you, my baby, so tightly in my arms
To share our love forever and keep you safe from harm
But that can never happen, you never saw the light of day
I couldn't keep you with me, I couldn't keep you here to stay

Now all I have is memories, fading as time passes by
I have the sense of failure, because I let you die
I can't visualise your features, which is so hard to bear
Because it makes me feel I didn't show you that I care

I cling on tightly to the pain, because it keeps you real
I'm scared to let it go in case it changes how I feel
I want to shed a tear for you, to accept that you are gone
But still I can't forgive myself, even though it's been so long

NUMB

Since I've felt this numb inside
It's been many years
And it's been even longer
Since I shed you any tears

But now I'm wallowing in nothingness
Time just drifting on
The empty void, that can't be filled
Simply because you're gone

The feeling of despair
The heavy aching of my heart
The suffocating sense of loss
It's tearing me apart

I thought I was done with grieving
Had forced the pain away
But now as I flounder in the past
It hurts like it was yesterday

RELEASE

Why is crying such a big deal
Maybe I'm scared to let myself feel
Sometimes I yearn to let the tears flow
But something inside won't let me let go
It's never the right time to let myself sob
I hold it all back, the pressure makes my head throb
I think that I've built it up for so long
If I let it out now, that connection is gone
If I take the release I might not feel so bad
But maybe I want to as that's all that I have

INSOMNIA

It's getting late, must be time for bed
It's time to relax and rest my poor head
So what is it that stops me from going upstairs
And seeking that time to forget troubles and cares

I know when I sleep my imagination is free
To merge all the thoughts, which are worrying me
I lose all control over what I let in my mind
How do I know what my subconscious might find

I stay up too late, and hope exhaustion will win
Hope to get far too tired for the dreams to begin
I snuggle under the covers and try not to think
If I make my mind blank, into sleep I might sink

I toss and I turn, I feel so wiped out
Yet still sleep eludes me, what's that all about
Time passes so slowly, a minute feels like an hour
I so long for release, but I don't have the power

At some point in the night I must finally sleep
But I never feel rested, it can't be that deep
The alarm rings in the morning, I'm already awake
I drag myself up, but how much more can I take

ALONE

Sometimes it feels like there's no one to care
Because the pain deep inside is so hard to share
For such a long time I've hidden the vulnerable me
It's just the tough outer shell that I let people see
I can't discard the mask behind which I hide
It's been there so long, held on with pride

I've been climbing so fast that I'm losing my grip
But I'm scared of where I'll land when I finally slip
Part of me wants to give in and let go
To have the courage to face whatever's below
Although I want to admit I can't get through by myself
I'm still clinging by fingertips to the edge of the shelf

I don't let anyone see when I'm not coping well
I hide away in my own private hell
Ask how I am and I'll say, "I'm fine"
Even if I feel I'm at the end of the line
I used to think all this meant I was strong
But now I can see that I got it all wrong

DREAMS

A lifetime of dreams, shattered in one day
I have to move on, I must find a way
To see you grow, I would have been so proud
Your face would've always stood out in a crowd

Dreams of laughter and fun
A new life just begun
Dreams of loving and sharing
A life full of caring

There are so many things that I wanted to see
You taking first steps, and smiling at me
I wanted to share everything in your life
Now all of these dreams have been cut like a knife

Dreams of laughter and fun
Our journey just begun
Dreams of loving and sharing
Now just despairing

So now a new dream, I will have to begin
I will learn from the pain, I will never give in
Your memory will always be locked in my heart
This gives me the strength to make a new start

EXPECTATIONS

I'm sitting here now trying to write
Need to clear my head, too tired to fight
My heart pounds so much it thumps in my ears
It shouldn't be like this after so many years
I should have moved on, been through this before
But with this built up emotion I'm rocked to the core
Don't expect to have to deal with this now
The truth of it is that I still don't know how

Explained to myself how I thought I should feel
Problem with that is, it doesn't actually heal
Can't tell anyone that things are not right
Like to keep it inside, locked up so tight
Bottling everything up deep inside
That's the way that I roll, but how long can I hide
I can't allow all this pain after so much time
I'll have to convince myself that I'm actually fine

TRYING TO LET GO

Driving home from work, feeling quite weary
Not much sleep last night, eyes are quite bleary
Nothing good on the radio, so I switch to a CD
Playing through songs that are all about me
Pull into the drive, find I'm the first one home
That's when it gets me, when I'm all on my own

I select a track and play it on repeat
Hoping that the words, will make me weep
I lay on my bed, face buried in my pillow
The tears feel so close, but I can't let them flow
I can't help but focus on the fact that I can't cry
I beat myself up trying so hard to work out why

I opened my mouth and tried to let out a scream
It wasn't convincing, so now I'm facing the screen
Pounding the keyboard, to banish my inner thoughts
It's my one safe haven when I'm so out of sorts
It doesn't ask questions, just lets me dwell
So I can be consumed, by my own private hell

The words are just tumbling, faster than I can type
It's the best way for me – I only express when I write
It seems to be the only way to regain my control
To push to the limit, then search for my soul
Not really that sure what I'm hoping to find
But my anxiety subsides and I reclaim my mind

THE MASK

I put on a smile as I walk down the street
Look straight ahead, not down at my feet
Projecting an image that I am carefree
Mask safely in place so no-one can see

I give the appearance I've nothing to hide
The turmoil I feel is locked deep inside
The need to be normal makes it too hard to show
Although time is passing, I still can't let go

I desperately want to let it all out
Weep buckets of tears, and scream and shout
But my body's on lockdown, refusing to play
So I'll keep up the pretence for at least one more day

I want you to believe that my mind is sound
It's important you think I've both feet on the ground
To keep my control is my one major task
So I'll continue to hide behind my emotionless mask

LOST GIRL

Lost girl, why do you look so sad
What's happened in your life to make you feel so bad
You're sitting here in silence with your head held in your hands
If you let me in I can help you understand

Lost girl, just staring into space
You need to look at life and find your special place
Don't shut yourself away, wrapped up in your pain
Let me help you learn to live your life again

Lost girl, so desperate to cry
You must accept what's past and not still question why
If you can forgive yourself you might see those tears
I'll be there beside you to help you overcome your fears

Lost girl, with a heavy heart
Stop striving for control and trust that you won't fall apart
You need to find the courage to turn your life around
I will be your guide and then the lost girl will be found

PART 2

This section of poems is about my journey as I discovered that there can be new hope and aspirations after loss and the realisation that all the pain and heartache you have suffered can have a positive effect on the way you choose to live the rest of your life.

THE ANGEL AND THE DEVIL

There's an angel on my shoulder trying to help me feel alright
But the devil on the other side is spoiling for a fight
I'm stuck here in the middle unsure which way to turn
I lean towards the angel to escape the devil's burn

The angel is inviting with the peace and calm that she exudes
She keeps a level head and helps control my moods
She looks me in the eye and says I've done no wrong
But I can't quite believe her because my baby's gone

The devil he is different, he makes me relive the pain
He prods at my subconscious and tells me I'm to blame
He teases me with ifs and buts and makes me doubt my mind
Sometimes he's so convincing, that to believe him I'm inclined

The angel comforts me and in her arms she holds me close
She tells me to respect myself and value those I love the most
But the devil he's so good at playing on my insecurities
He can grab my heart and twist until it brings me to my knees

So you'd think it should be obvious, the angel's got the devil beat
But there's still a part inside of me that's drawn towards the heat
I need to have the confidence to let the angel help me soar
And trust without the devil I won't feel cold right through my core

THE ANGEL AND THE DEVIL – PART II

The angel isn't happy about my indecision
She thinks that the devil is keeping me imprisoned
She tries extra hard, she's really upped her game
She's determined that the devil won't drive me insane

But the devil he is angry, at the angel he now glares
He reminds me of my loss and tells me no one cares
He doesn't like the angel questioning his blatant lies
He wants me to believe him, but I've opened up my eyes

The devil pulls out all the stops to try and tighten up his grip
He can sense my mood is shifting and he tries to make me slip
He will have to work much harder – I'm not listening any longer
He can't convince me easily now I'm feeling so much stronger

The angel she encourages me to face up to my fears
She helps me believe my love won't fade with the passing years
She wants me to accept I won't forget you, without the constant pain
For she's worried that the devil will try and take control again

I'm exhausted from the effort of deciding which to choose
Whichever way I turn there's always something I will lose
From the angel's guidance, I've found some peace inside
And from the devil's taunting, I've found the strength to survive

I summoned all my courage, and from them both I stepped away
I was pleasantly surprised to find the world has colour, not just grey
I've discovered I can trust myself, I don't need either anymore
Now I'm following my own path, whatever life may have in store

INSANITY

I have now found a bitter sweet sanctuary
I have reached an acceptance that some things can't be
I don't still blame myself, or try to justify why
I've learnt to live with the fact that you died

I can think of you now with more love than pain
And days are now filled with more sunshine than rain
Yet deep inside there's a doubt hounding me
Perhaps I'm still hiding what I don't want to see

The time that we had was so precious, but so brief
Clouded failing memories can consume me with grief
Yet simple things now can mean so much more
So I live for today, not what the future might store

Contradicting thoughts going round in my brain
Does that make me human, or does it mean I'm insane

THE WOUND

Inside my heart is wounded, I don't know if it will heal
I'm astounded by the intensity and depth of pain I feel
Time is dragging by so slowly, you're all that's on my mind
To put one foot before the other takes all the courage I can find

Now other thoughts are creeping in, no longer kept at bay
The wound is starting to mend and I'm scared you'll go away
I scratch blindly at the edges as I try to keep it raw
It feels like I'm betraying you if it doesn't stay as sore

My mind is laced with guilt if I think of anything but you
Because you should be here with me in everything I do
But no matter how I fight it, the healing just won't stop
A scab forms over the abyss, a protective layer on top

The scab is almost gone and the pain has faded too
But I'm no longer scared because I know I won't forget you
For I have a permanent reminder, the wound has left a scar
So I will always remember you, no matter where you are

SOMETIMES

Sometimes it's easier to laugh and joke
Can't show the hurt, in case you choke
Sometimes it's hard to keep up the pretence
When nothing seems to make much sense
Can't let anyone see the pain
That just goes against the grain
Got to keep it deep inside
Trying so very hard to hide

Sometimes the world seems so unfair
People pass by without a care
All caught up in their own dreams
Yours are torn apart at the seams
Sometimes you think all hope is gone
Can't see a reason to carry on
You can torment yourself with blame
But the result is still the same

Sometimes you have to give in to the tears
You can't hide from all your fears
Sometimes you have to walk right through the pain
Then you can start to face the world again
It may take a long, long time
But in the end you'll be just fine
So don't ever give up your hope
It will get easier to cope

Sometimes life seems such a trial
But one day you will learn to smile
You can't rush to feel ok
But when the sometimes become less times
You know you're on your way

LITTLE TEDDY BEAR

There's a lonely little teddy bear, peering through the glass
He longs to come inside, but he's far too scared to ask
He wanders round the house, afraid to knock the door
He wants to be accepted, but he really isn't sure

The teddy is not perfect, his ear is slightly torn
His fur is wearing thin, and he's looking quite forlorn
He looks in through the window and gives a great big sigh
The fire looks so warm, but he feels so sad that he could cry

Then the front door opens, the child comes out to play
Teddy doesn't want to be seen, so he tries to sneak away
He is spotted by the child, so he braces for rejection
He wants her to go away, but she's running in his direction

She grabs hold of him, and hugs him really tight
She doesn't seem to care that he really looks a sight
"I can't believe I've found you, I thought that you were lost"
"But I never gave up looking, I kept my fingers crossed"

Then the teddy realises love stands the test of time
It doesn't matter to the girl that he's all covered in grime
She looks beyond the surface and just sees her favourite bear
He's only got so tatty because she takes him everywhere

THE ONION

I took an onion from the cupboard and put it on the side
I stared at it for ages, whilst trying to decide
Then I found a little confidence and peeled the skin away
If came off quite easily – a good start, I'm on the way

I gazed at my onion, sitting there without its skin
If I break through a layer, I know it will start to sting
Tentatively I peel again – I hope it's not too strong
I try to do it quickly so it doesn't take too long

That first layer wasn't so hard, my confidence is growing
The reality wasn't as bad as the seed my mind was sowing
I take off a couple more layers, each one is thicker than the last
I need to focus on getting to the centre, not what's already passed

I don't know if I can go much further, I'm really getting in a state
It's taken over all my senses, and my mind has shut the gate
I'm struggling to breathe, my eyes are watering like crazy
I try to keep my focus, but everything is getting hazy

My body gets defensive and my mind withdraws inside
I can't go on like this forever, but right now I need to hide
I glance back at the onion, so small, but causing so much pain
I don't want to let it beat me, I know I have to face up to it again

I need some assistance, so it's gloves and chewing gum
If I stand a chance of winning I have to overcome
With my new found protection the odds are in my favour
I no longer fear the onion, now instead its taste I savour

THE JOURNEY

Staring into emptiness, lost inside of my own mind
I don't know what I'm thinking and I don't know what I'll find
I thought I'd handled losing you so many years ago
But now I find myself back in the past feeling really low

I can't keep my focus on normal daily tasks
And I can't control how long this state will last
I'm totally consumed, like I still need to grieve
With suffocating numbness that makes it hard to breathe

It's time that I accepted I need help to work this out
But asking is a problem, something I don't know how to go about
I have to summon up the courage to admit that I can't cope
And take that first tiny step so I can find new hope

Time for my first session, my anxiety is strong
What if this is a mistake, what if I've got it wrong
I'm feeling very nervous – I find it hard to share
But I know that I will have to if I want to get somewhere

So I take a deep breath and enter through the door
I've envisioned this for days but still I feel unsure
An hour passed so quickly, felt like I'd only just got going
The time just disappeared without me even knowing

When I talked about your birth there was a wobble in my voice
I tried hard not to show it, but I didn't have a choice
My arms were folded tightly, my body giving me away
As I tried to hide the effect on me of remembering your day

As I'm driving home it feels like there is some light
I'm glad I found the courage, the decision to go was right
Now I am concerned I have to get through another week
Before I go again and once more have the chance to speak

Sessions come and go with plenty of frustration
When I can't find the words I need I'm filled with irritation
A thousand conversations in my head of what I want to say
All uselessly forgotten when I get there on the day

I curse my defensive barriers, my emotions I can't show
Ask me how things make me feel, I'll tell you I don't know
My mind goes completely blank – I don't know where to begin
But all I want so desperately is to let somebody in

I sink down in depression and nothing seems worthwhile
I feel completely broken – I can't even raise a smile
I immerse myself in negatives, and become so self-obsessed
Even the simplest issues seem to get me really stressed

The sessions are a lifeline, when I'm so full of self-doubt
My counsellor reminds me of what life should be about
She encourages my confidence and helps me clearly see
She makes me think about myself and whom I want to be

Gradually as time moves on I don't feel so much despairing pain
But then I start to panic that without it I will lose you once again
I thought the physical reaction stopped us from drifting apart
But I'm glad that I was wrong because you're safe inside my heart

It's been a long hard trip down a very rocky path
But I know I'm getting there – I've remembered how to laugh
For counselling I will always be grateful eternally
Now I can enjoy my life as I continue on its journey

WISHING

I would swim across the ocean
Or reach the stars up in the sky
If it meant I could go back in time
And that you didn't die
I would climb Mount Everest
Or fly to outer space
If I could have just one more chance
To see your little face

I have wished a billion times
I've made a silent plea
But now I have to face the fact
That some things just can't be
I won't pretend the pain has gone
Or regrets have slipped away
But wishing I could change the past
Won't bring you back to stay

So instead of desperate longing
For the impossible to come true
I will value how my life has changed
Because I once knew you
As I journey on through life
You will be right by my side
And whenever things get tough
Your love will be my guide

ALWAYS

You are my little angel, now in heaven above
You touched my life so briefly, but gave me so much love
I never knew, my child, that I could feel so strong
I tried hard not to show it, now I admit that I was wrong

You will always be my baby, my special little boy
Although you've caused me heartache, you've brought me so much joy
I am honoured to have known you, to keep you in my heart
We will always be together, even though we are apart

You will always be remembered, I will love you every day
You will always share my future, it has to be that way
I know I'll still feel pain and hurt, but now I'm more prepared
My feelings make me strong, not weak, and now I'm not so scared

So now my precious little one, it's time that I said thank you
You've taught me much about myself, and everything I do
I've learnt to appreciate, you've opened up my eyes
I just wish I'd learnt another way, and not because you died

I know that one day, once again, we will be together
But until then I'll hold you close, my love will last forever
In this I can take comfort, to see me through my days
Now I can start to live again, for you are with me always

THE FUTURE

I couldn't see into the future
I couldn't see past all the pain
I didn't think there'd ever be a time
That I could enjoy my life again

I never knew that I could think of you
Without that tearing at my heart
And if I lost the agony of grief
I thought that we'd grow further apart

But now I know that I was wrong
It's not pain that keeps us together
It's our love that holds us close
And will stay with me forever

No longer do I dread each day
Or wonder how I will get through
I don't know what the future holds
But I will make it because of you

PART 3

Coping with grief can be harder at certain times such as future pregnancy, anniversaries and Christmas. These poems all relate to these occasions.

REFLECTIONS

The time has arrived that you should have been born
And as I sit here staring at the sea all forlorn
I can't ignore the pain in my chest
You should be here now, not laid to rest

I'm sitting here hoping that at last I can cry
But alas once again my eyes are still dry
The best I can do is sit here and write
Because all of my feelings are locked up so tight

Because I can't show it, don't think I don't care
Wherever you are now, I'd love to be there
But I can't leave this world yet, of others I must think
So I'll pull myself together and step back from the brink

ANOTHER BABY

I want another baby
But I'm scared to even try
I can't guarantee survival
What if another dies

If the worst were to happen
I don't know how I'd cope
Losing one precious baby
Has made me lose all hope

I have to overcome the fear
Because the broodiness is strong
Now I've made my mind up
I hope it doesn't take too long

Each month lasts forever
As I wait for the line to turn to blue
But the moment that it does
I don't know what I will do

There's bitter disappointment
If the test says not this time
But also there's some relief
That no life is on the line

So many mixed emotions
I want another child so much
But I can't convince myself
I'll ever feel his touch

A NEW ARRIVAL

So now it's really happening, the test has turned to blue
My hopes are now reality, I want to plan my life with you
But I panic when I think of all the things that could go wrong
Why on earth does pregnancy have to last so long

That you are growing inside of me is so hard to believe
I want to feel excited, but for your brother I still grieve
I should be filled with elation, but instead all I feel is fear
Because I don't know if we'll make it, the future isn't clear

I long for the naivety, to trust everything will be alright
But I struggle to believe that I will ever hold you tight
I can't imagine for a moment that you have a chance to live
And it rips my heart out because I've so much love to give

Every minute seems like an hour, each hour is like a day
I hold my breath at every scan until I know that you're ok
Each little twinge or funny feeling sets me in a spin
I'm desperate for you to get here so our future can begin

We're passing all the milestones, I almost dare to hope
Please don't leave me now, I don't think that I could cope
I love my big fat belly, and don't care that I can't see my feet
But I long for your safe arrival – I can't wait for us to meet

Finally you're born, perfect, alive and well
I can't believe we've made it through nine months of hell
I haven't dared to dream of this – you safely in my arms
Now I swear I will do all I can to keep you safe from harm

TIME

It's been two years since we were parted
It sounds like it's so long
Yet it feels like only yesterday
That I was told that you were gone

Such a rollercoaster of emotion
Knowing you has brought
I didn't know how much you meant
But still you're in my every thought

When I think of all the time that's passed
I feel I should be moving on
I can't believe such pain's still there
I don't feel so very strong

I'm scared of all my time ahead
In which I can't watch you grow
How can I make it through my life
When there's so much I'll never know

But I do know that I won't forget you
Though it doesn't always seem that way
I'll cling to our few memories
To get me through another day

EACH NEW DAY

Three years ago my world was blown apart
When a scan discovered no beat of your heart
For over four months you grew inside of me
It was sheer devastation to find your life would not be

When I knew you had died, I couldn't believe it was true
My future, my dreams were all built around you
I couldn't accept what I didn't want to know
Because that would mean I would have to let go

I struggled with the physical and mental pain
Too scared to sleep and live through it again
I tortured myself with guilt and self-blame
And some of my actions still fill me with shame

Now I have realised that I will always love you
And you are always with me whatever I do
So now I hold you close, instead of pushing you away
I can't change the past, but I can face each new day

A CHRISTMAS MESSAGE

Dear Mum and Dad, I know I'm not there
So I'm sending this message, to let you know that I care
At this special time, full of loving and giving
I want to remind you, in your heart I'm still living

Now is a time to laugh and celebrate
I want you to be happy, don't hesitate
I am the angel on top of the tree
You don't have to worry, you won't forget me

When you feel low, I want you to remember
I'm always with you, come June or December
Because of me, you know the strength of love
Take comfort in this, when you look up above

I will never leave you, I'm here to stay
So please don't be sad on this Christmas Day
Because what better gift could you have than me
Safe where I belong, in your heart and memory

CHRISTMAS WISHES

Christmas is here once again, and another year has passed by
I told you, you wouldn't forget me, and now I'm telling you why
Although I'm not with you in body, I am in your heart and mind
I'll be with you wherever you are, whatever your future might find

So what do I want for Christmas, I've written a list you see
I want you all to be happy, not sad because you don't have me
I want you to laugh and be merry, without that feeling of shame
It doesn't mean you don't love me, just that there's a little less pain

On Christmas Eve look up to the stars and watch the reindeer fly
I'll be sitting next to Santa, way up there in the sky
So don't feel sad and lonely, that you can't hold me tight
I'm sending you a great big hug to keep you warm at night

ALONE AT CHRISTMAS

All the hustle and the bustle
Shoppers crowding in the street
Busy buying all their gifts
To make Christmas a real treat

Children running everywhere
Full of excitement and joy
All they want for Christmas
Is a brand new shiny toy

Christmas trees with fairy lights
Crackers, mulled wine and mince pies
All the trimmings make it perfect
But they don't see it through your eyes

They don't see the pain your feeling
Or the loneliness inside
Or know that you can't celebrate
Because your baby died

At this special time of giving
You have so much love to share
And yet your heart is ripped apart
And no one seems to care

ANGEL WINGS

Christmas time is here and snow is all around
Frosty white snowflakes are covering the ground
Decorations going up and lights around the tree
My brother hangs a bauble especially for me

It's nice that they remember, I feel part of the family
I wish that I was there, but I know that just can't be
I want to hug them all and let them feel my love
Sometimes it's just so hard, only looking from above

That I'm watching over them, I hope that they will know
Because I've made some angel wings outside in the snow
I hope they'll look out of the window and see that I was there
And remember that their angel is with them everywhere

PART 4

This section is about the charity SPRING. These are poems that I have written about events organised and support offered by the charity. I have included these because the help I have received myself has been invaluable and I feel very strongly that its good work should be recognised. Counselling provided by SPRING has played a huge part in helping me find my way forward and inspired many of the poems in this book; therefore I have also included the poem I wrote for my counsellor Cindy as thanks for all her help and support.

THE SPRING SUITE

The bereavement suite is such a special place
When your world has collapsed and you need your own space
It's a place where nobody should ever have to be
For it means that in life you know tragedy

The reason it exists, may be very sad
But because it is here, I am very glad
For nothing this bad, before has happened to me
And it helped me so much to have this sanctuary

The suite has been built with such detail and care
With genuine concern for you, while you are there
It's not like a hospital, but far more homely
The comfort it offers, makes life seem less lonely

The suite is an asset that should always be treasured
For any help to ease grief can never be measured
When our dreams ceased to be, and the future wasn't bright
The SPRING suite gave us, our first new ray of light

SPRING OPEN SUPPORT MEETINGS

When your precious baby dies, and you're struggling to cope
You crave for understanding, and need to find some hope
When everything seems pointless and your whole world is caving in
You don't know which way to turn, or where you should begin

There are others out there who are feeling just the same
You can share your deepest thoughts and you won't feel quite so insane
You will be able to take comfort, you don't have to face this on your own
It can make it so much easier to know you're not alone

That is why SPRING meetings have more value than I can say
You can talk or you can listen and it will help you in some way
So if you're searching for some solace, then I urge you, come along
Sharing helps to ease the pain when your little one is gone

COUNSELLING

When my little angel died, my naivety left too
He didn't get a chance at life – I didn't know what to do
I tried so hard to carry on, but inside I lived a lie
I battled with the turmoil, my days just drifting by

I decided to seek counsel to help me straighten out my mind
When you probe into your subconscious it's surprising what you find
Sometimes the simplest question changed the way that I was thinking
Or just some reassurance stopped the feeling I was sinking

Being able to talk openly without being scared of how you seem
Proved to be invaluable when I had no self-esteem
I needed someone else to help me tolerate my pain
I talked through all my feelings, the guilt and the self-blame

Now I'm done with just existing, it's good to feel alive
I no longer have to question, I know I will survive
I've found my self-confidence and life I now enjoy
I appreciate what I have, although I still miss my little boy

Without having counselling I wouldn't be there yet
I would still be floundering, living with so much regret
Sometimes when it's so dark, it's hard to find the light
That's when you need a little guidance to help you ease your plight

THE SNOWDROP GARDEN

A special garden in the grounds at Poole Cemetery
So many tiny graves, for so many lost babies
You will be overwhelmed as you enter through the gate
The reality of shattered dreams is so hard to contemplate
Each little grave is tended with so much thought and care
So many gifts adorn them, you can feel love everywhere
There are flowers, teddies, windmills, to name but just a few
A perfect place to remember the babies we never knew
There are benches you can sit on, whilst you reminisce
To help to ease the pain you feel for the little one you miss

SNOWDROP WALK

Snowdrops in the woodland, life's fragility compound
A stark, poignant reminder, of why we're all gathered around
A cold, frosty winter's day, the grass is tipped an icy white
The wind is nipping at your face, balloons are ready to take flight

Sunlight is peeping through the clouds, a promise of a brighter day
Special messages are written and the balloons are on their way
Off on their own adventures, they start to float up high
Disappearing in the distance, soaring through the sky

Now the mood is sombre, lost in thoughts all of your own
The balloons are out of sight and suddenly you feel alone
But remember they're just on a different path, not gone forever
One day those paths will cross again and once more you'll be together

WAVE OF LIGHT

A candle's fragile flicker
A glimmer in the dark
As we all gather together
In the gardens at Poole Park

Lost in our own memories
Emotions running high
As we remember all our babies
Whilst we look up to the sky

Surrounded by the sadness
Engulfed in our own pain
Hoping that the time will come
When we can smile again

Take comfort in this moment
Feel compassion everywhere
You don't have to be alone
Because everyone here cares

If we take each fragile candle
Together they burn so bright
They show our babies lit our lives
In a global wave of light

CHRISTMAS SERVICE

On a cold wintry day as Christmas drew near
We gathered together for the babies we hold dear
The tiny little chapel was packed to the brim
It was a bit of a squeeze to fit everyone in

We shared carols and poems whilst our thoughts were our own
A time for reflecting, but not being alone
Emotions ran high, and a few tears were shed
As we sang, "Away in a manger, no crib for his bed"

After the service we visited the tree
Where we hung our messages for all to see
We lit candles, ate cookies and drank mulled wine
As we remembered our babies at Christmas time

CINDY

It seems hard to believe that our time has reached an end
It doesn't seem that long ago I felt I was going round the bend
I didn't like the fact that I had lost my self-control
I was after a quick fix, but you made me search my soul

You persuaded me to write to help get round my mental block
So I wrote fifteen thousand words at all hours of the clock
But even so I didn't write what I was feeling at the time
Luckily for me you're good at reading between the lines

Although at times I struggled to find the words to say
You encouraged me to look at things in a different way
Although I still have barriers, I've never opened up so much
Which in itself is a miracle, you really have the touch

You wouldn't let me wallow, when I hit the depths of despair
And you didn't give up on me when I couldn't share
You indulged my love of music and got what the lyrics mean to me
And you brought me back to my senses when I was losing Rosie

You found me precious pictures to remind me of my son
To help ease my regret that of him I don't have one
You helped me to believe that pain isn't all I have to feel
I can remember him with love and he is every bit as real

So I'm writing this to thank you for all you've done for me
Without all your input I don't know where I would be
I know I've been a challenge, but I'm so glad that we met
For you've helped me turn my life around, which I won't ever forget

PART 5

This final part came about because one evening whilst I was working on a poem, my 13 year old son, Ryan came into the study. I showed him the draft of this book and he asked if he could write a poem to be included in it. It got me thinking about the fact that Dominic was a brother to Ryan and Adam and a son to Mick as well as me and that we all feel his loss. I decided that I wanted us all to contribute, so this book will be a treasured memory of Dominic for all of us. My 9 year old, Adam has also written a poem and my husband, Mick painted the picture for the front cover of the teddy bears I bought for each of my three boys when I was expecting Adam. He is also incredibly good at finding the right titles for my poems.

This last section has just four poems. One from each of my two boys and two from me called, "Precious Bundle" and, "To Love Your Child". These for me are about the depth of love I feel for my children and the lengths I would go to, to protect them. They epitomise why it is so hard to deal with losing a child and therefore, in essence, why this book exists. In my opinion there is no greater love than that which you feel for your children.

MY BROTHER

Dazzling
Outstanding
Missed every day
Incredible
Nice to be your brother
Infinitely loved
Coolest brother ever

Written by Adam Lambert (age 9)

ONE OF MANY

Dear brother, it's time to face reality,
You were a fighter, but you've lost your vitality.
However, I know that you will not be lonesome,
As with the other many children, you'll find it awesome.

Remember that you are one of many,
A whisper in a loud cacophony.
A baby fish in a tranquil ocean,
An important movement in a brilliant motion.

A single droplet in a mass monsoon,
A small breeze in a giant typhoon.
A tiny star in the vast night sky,
A sad teardrop in a million goodbyes.

A working ant in a big colony,
A note of music in a beautiful symphony.
A speck of dust on the wide, open floor,
A quiet squeak in a mighty roar.

A primed arrow in a packed quiver,
A little shudder in a colossus shiver.
A spectacular brother,
In a sea of others.

So don't be sad little boy,
Go out, make friends and enjoy.
To find more children you won't have to stray far,
But don't worry, we'll always know which one you are.

Written by Ryan Lambert (age 13)

PRECIOUS BUNDLE

Oh precious little bundle
You take my breath away
I've been waiting for this moment
I've been longing for this day

All that I've imagined
Doesn't even come near
To the intensity of feelings
Now that I hold you dear

Your gorgeous little face
Wide eyes, looking up at me
Filled with unending love
For all the world to see

Your tiny little fingers
So firm in their grasp
You're everything I wanted
There's nothing more I ask

To me you are my purpose
The reason that I exist
There's no one more important
I hope you get the gist

You're my perfect little miracle
All my dreams come true
Whatever challenges I face in life
Our love will see me through

TO LOVE YOUR CHILD

A child is the most precious gift
From the moment you conceive
Your feelings are so much stronger
Than you ever could believe

When you first see your child
There are no words to describe
The overwhelming love
That you feel so deep inside

An instinctual urge to protect
You would sacrifice your life
Your love is unconditional
Even when they cause you strife

You nurse them when they're sick
And comfort them through pain
You laugh with them and share good times
That you can relive time and time again

Soon they're getting older
They don't depend on you as much
But wherever their life takes them
You will always keep in touch

EPILOGUE

I will always be sad that I didn't get the chance to watch Dominic grow, and I often wonder what his personality would be like, but I am also very happy that he touched my life. Although he is not here in person, he has had such a great impact on my life. He has changed my outlook and made me appreciate and value everything so much more. I have never known such excruciating pain and distress as that of having your child taken from you before he has even taken a breath, but if I were given the choice to go through it again knowing the anguish and suffering I would experience, or for him to never have existed, there would be no contest.

I don't think the sense of longing for what can never be, or regret that he didn't make it will ever go away completely, and I'm ok with that. As time passes the positive feelings have gradually become dominant. When I think of Dominic now, I feel an overwhelming warmth and love, tinged with just a hint of sadness. He is one of my three precious, cherished children, whom have made me the better person I am today.